NATURE
SPOTTERS

WHAT CAN YOU SPOT ON THE SEASHORE?

What wonderful wildlife will you discover on the seashore? See which of the 170 species featured in this book you can spot, and tick them off. When you have found 50 or more, you will have earned your top Nature Spotters certificate! Simply fill it in, tear it out from the back of the book and pin it up on your wall.

The book is divided into themes such as fish, shells, seaweed and birds. Test your nature knowledge with the quiz questions at the start of every section, and then turn to page 76 to see how many you have answered correctly.

CRUSTACEANS

Seashore life occurs in zones. You can see the zones at low tide, with the upper zone being the furthest from the sea and the lower zone being the closest. Crustaceans are found in all zones. They have three body segments, two pairs of antennae and jointed legs. Most also have a shell for protection.

Two out of the six animals shown below are crustaceans. Do you know, or can you guess, which ones they are?

Sea slater

Garden snail

Orange-tip

Marsh frog

Rose chafer

Lobster

BARNACLE

Barnacles grip seashore rocks, protected from the battering waves by a tough shell. Inside, the soft-bodied animals are safely cemented to the rock. At high tide, they extend feathery legs to catch food.

DID YOU KNOW?
Like many other marine animals, barnacles start life as spiky larvae which drift in the sea, before settling on rocks.

SHORE:	Rocky
ZONE:	Upper to lower
SEEN:	All year round
SHELL:	Pointed; 4 or 6 joined sections
FEEDS ON:	Food filtered from the water
SIZE:	Up to 2 cm high

SHORE CRAB

This crab, which can be brown, orange or greenish, is the one you are most likely to discover in rockpools or among seaweed. It uses the five legs on each side of its body to scuttle sideways across the sand.

SHORE:	All types of shore
ZONE:	Middle
SEEN:	Spring to autumn
SHELL:	Variable colour
FEEDS ON:	Wide range of prey
SIZE:	Up to 8 cm across the shell

DID YOU KNOW?
A crab's pincers can be different sizes – big ones are good for crushing and smaller ones are better for cutting things.

OTHER CRABS

VELVET SWIMMING CRAB

This species lives under rocks and has red eyes. If it feels threatened, it rears up and waves its pincers around. No wonder its nickname is the devil crab!

EDIBLE CRAB

When young, an edible crab will shelter in rockpools, but a larger one stays further offshore. Its smooth brown shell has crinkled edges, like a Cornish pasty.

HERMIT CRAB

A hermit crab lacks a shell, so it searches for an empty one to move into and then wears it on its back. If attacked, it pulls its legs inside its adopted shell.

SPIDER CRAB

These crabs have long, spindly legs and a spiny shell up to 20 cm wide. They prefer deep water, but in summer they visit the shallows to moult their shells.

BROWN SHRIMP

Shrimps spend much of the time half-buried in the seabed in shallow water, with only their antennae and goggle eyes showing. They are well camouflaged against sand or mud. So if you spot one, well done!

SHORE:	Sandy or muddy
ZONE:	Middle and lower
SEEN:	All year round
SHELL:	Sandy brown with darker spots
FEEDS ON:	Scraps and pieces of floating food
SIZE:	Up to 9 cm

DID YOU KNOW?
These shrimps change colour to match their background. If spooked, they will suddenly shoot backwards.

COMMON PRAWN

Prawns dart about in rockpools and shallow water. When they stop they seem to disappear, as their bodies are see-through. They can be found in large rockpools, hiding in corners or under rocks.

DID YOU KNOW?
Prawns can be very curious animals – if you stay still and are patient, they may come to inspect you.

SHORE:	Rocky
ZONE:	Upper to lower
SEEN:	All year round
SHELL:	Transparent with dark lines
FEEDS ON:	Scraps of floating food
SIZE:	Up to 11 cm

SHELLS

Shells come in all shapes, sizes and colours. They are made by soft-bodied creatures called molluscs, which live inside them for protection. Double shells are in two parts, joined by a hinge with a muscle to open and shut them. Others are single shells, often a long cone or a spiral, like garden snails.

Shellfish is the name for animals that live inside shells. Can you guess which of these animals feed on shellfish?

Otter

Oystercatcher

Turkey

Black-throated diver

Humpback whale

Sea turtle

COMMON COCKLE

A cockle has a fan-shaped shell and burrows into sand, around 5 cm below the surface. As the tide comes in, it opens its shell to suck in water and extract food particles, then squirts out the waste water.

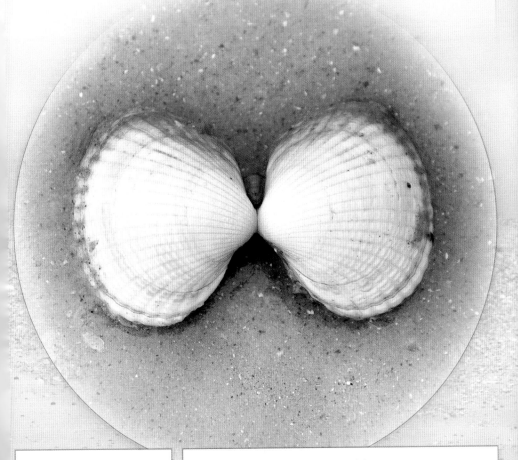

SHORE:	Sandy or muddy
ZONE:	Middle and lower
SEEN:	All year round
SHELL:	Creamy white with lots of ridges
FEEDS ON:	Food filtered from the water
SIZE:	Up to 5 cm across the shell

BANDED WEDGE SHELL

This pretty shell has bands of pink, yellow or brown on a pale background, and a glossy surface. It digs a shallow burrow in sandy beaches and bays, and its empty shells are easy to find.

SHORE:	Sandy
ZONE:	Middle and lower
SEEN:	All year round
SHELL:	White with coloured bands
FEEDS ON:	Food filtered from the water
SIZE:	Up to 3.5 cm long

DID YOU KNOW?
The edges of the hinged shell lock together to stop predators from getting in. If disturbed, it burrows into the sand.

RAZOR SHELL

These long shells look like the traditional razors used by men's hairdressers. Razor shells live in vertical burrows dug in the wet sand, and storms can hurl masses of them up the beach.

SHORE:	Sandy
ZONE:	Lower
SEEN:	All year round
SHELL:	White with brown areas
FEEDS ON:	Food filtered from the water
SIZE:	Up to 20 cm long

BLUE MUSSEL

Mussels grow on wave-splashed rocks at the base of cliffs and on rocky reefs, where they pack together in clumps called mussel beds. They attach to rocks by means of tough, sticky threads called beards.

SHORE:	Rocky
ZONE:	Middle and lower
SEEN:	All year round
SHELL:	Bluish-black or dark purple
FEEDS ON:	Food filtered from the water
SIZE:	Up to 10 cm long

DID YOU KNOW?
Mussel beards are five times stronger than human tendons – the tough tissue connecting our muscles and bones.

OTHER DOUBLE SHELLS

TELLIN

Look for these pretty shells in the sand or mud of estuaries. They are a type of clam and most are white, pinkish or orange, with neat bands of darker colours.

PIDDOCK

Piddocks have long, white, wing-shaped shells. They drill holes in soft rocks to live in, and from here they extend their soft body parts into the seawater to feed.

OTTER SHELL

These large, double shells burrow in sandy shores, digging down as much as 40 cm. They have long feeding tubes to reach food at the surface of the seabed.

OYSTER

A popular food since ancient times, oysters are becoming rare owing to pollution and over-picking. Conservation schemes are restoring them to some areas.

SINGLE SHELLS

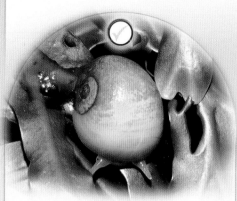

FLAT PERIWINKLE
These little shells live amongst seaweed on the lower shore and may be orange, yellow, green or brown. They are a type of sea snail and they graze on seaweed.

AUGER SHELL
Auger shells are beautiful cones up to 3 cm long, with deep grooves that spiral around the outside. Search for them on both sandy and muddy shores.

TOPSHELLS
Shaped like spinning tops, each of these pretty small shells contains a soft-bodied snail. Topshells are found on all rocky shores, where they graze on algae.

COMMON WHELK
Whelks are large, carnivorous sea snails, and this common species has a creamy white, conical shell up to 10 cm long. You may also find its empty egg cases.

DOG WHELK
Look for dog whelks on rocky shores. They feed on other molluscs, drilling holes into the shells of their prey in order to suck out the soft flesh inside.

COMMON LIMPET
Limpets clamp down on rocks and look like tiny grey volcanoes. At high tide, they slide over the rocky surfaces to graze on algae, returning later to the same spot.

SLIPPER LIMPET
These molluscs have oval shells that stack together, so appear to be a single animal. Although they live mostly offshore, the empty shells get washed up on beaches.

SPOTTED COWRIE
Cowries are tiny, and their pretty pink shell has delicate ridges and three dark splodges. You are most likely to see them on rocky shores in western Britain.

BEACHCOMBING

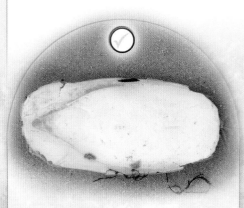

CUTTLEFISH BONE

Cuttlefish bones look like little white surfboards. These special structures are a type of internal shell that helps to support the bodies of squid-like cuttlefish.

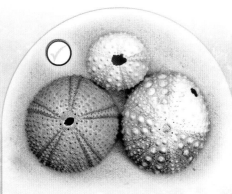

SEA-URCHIN TEST

A living sea urchin is prickly, but when it dies its spines fall off. They leave white bumps on the small satsuma-shaped skeleton, which is known as a "test".

MERMAID'S PURSE

These mysterious leathery objects are the empty egg cases of two kinds of fish – small sharks and skates. Each purse was home once to a developing baby fish.

GOOSE BARNACLE

Look for groups of these pale grey shells stuck to logs, rope, plastic or other debris washed up by rough seas. Each shell has a thick stalk to cling on with.

COMMON WHELK
EGG CASE

The empty egg cases of this sea snail often wash up on beaches. Inside the papery capsules were once hundreds of whelk eggs.

CRAB'S PINCER

Crabs moult their armoured shell many times as they grow, and the empty ones are a common sight on seashores. You might also come across a crab pincer.

DRIFTWOOD

Branches and pieces of wood that wash up onto the seashore are usually bleached by the sun and salt, and worn smooth by the force of the waves.

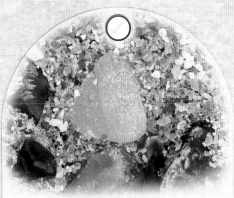

SEA GLASS

Sea glass starts life as jars or bottles floating in the ocean. These are broken into ever smaller pieces by the power of the sea's current and waves.

Fish

Our shores are valuable homes to everything from tiddlers to sharks. Many of these creatures are small and hide amongst seaweed, under rocks or half-buried in sand – with a bit of searching you may spot them. Larger fish stay further out to sea and are easier to see from cliffs or piers or on boat trips.

Do you know which of the creatures below are fish and which are mammals? The answers might surprise you.

Perch

Pike

Brown trout

Mackerel

Dolphins

Carp

BASKING SHARK

These gentle giants are the world's second-largest fish, but are no danger to humans. They visit in summer and cruise slowly at the surface with jaws wide open to hoover up vast quantities of tiny prey.

DID YOU KNOW?
This shark, which weighs as much as four cars, filters two million litres of water an hour through its gills.

FOUND:	Coasts of Ireland and west Britain
ZONE:	Sheltered bays or around islands
SEEN:	May to August
FEEDS ON:	Tiny floating plankton
FEATURES:	Triangular fin shows above water
SIZE:	Up to 12 m

COMMON BLENNY

With its flattened body, this little fish can squeeze into the tightest of spaces to hide. Also known as the shanny, it doesn't have scales, unlike most fish. Instead, its body is covered in slime for protection.

FOUND:	Under rocks and in rockpools
ZONE:	Middle
SEEN:	Spring to autumn
FEEDS ON:	Worms, sea snails and crustaceans
FEATURES:	Long, flat body; single fin on back
SIZE:	Up to 13 cm

DID YOU KNOW?
Thanks to their slimy bodies, blennies can live out of water, providing they can find a damp place out of the sun.

SAND GOBY

The mottled colour of this tiny fish hides it well in its sandy home.
Look for the bulging eyes and spiny fins at the front of its body. The
chunky head may be a quarter of the creature's total length.

DID YOU KNOW?
*The sand goby has
many enemies, from
gulls to larger fish. To
escape its predators, it
buries itself in the sand.*

FOUND:	Shallow pools on sandy shores
ZONE:	Middle and lower
SEEN:	All year
FEEDS ON:	Worms and shrimps
FEATURES:	Huge head; two fins on its back
SIZE:	Up to 10 cm

BUTTERFISH

Butterfish are thin and ribbon-like. Their bodies are slimy and have
no scales, which makes them extremely slippery. Unusually for fish,
both the male and the female may take it in turns to guard the eggs.

FOUND:	Under rocks and amongst seaweed
ZONE:	Lower
SEEN:	All year
FEEDS ON:	Small crustaceans and worms
FEATURES:	Long fin on back; black spots
SIZE:	Up to 25 cm

DID YOU KNOW?
*Their slippery bodies
make them almost
impossible for humans
to catch, but otters have
no problem.*

OTHER FISH

GREY MULLET
Mullet are medium-sized sea fish which move around in large, silvery shoals. Good places to spot them include river mouths, marinas and harbours.

ROCK GOBY
This little fish has a huge head for its size and a hairy-looking nose. You usually find it hiding in rockpools, under boulders or in the shallows in the sea.

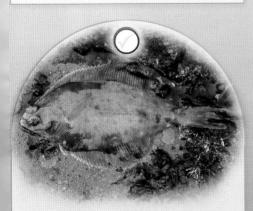

DAB
Dab are one of several flatfish found along sandy shores. Their peculiar body shape is perfect for hiding on the seabed, with only their eyes above the sand.

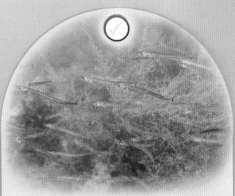

SAND EEL
Sand eels are the favourite food of many seabirds – you commonly see them lined up in the beaks of puffins! They live half-buried in seabeds offshore.

OTHER SEA ANIMALS

Among the many sea creatures you might find living along the coast, there are spiny animals such as starfish and sea urchins; and two groups that fire venom darts to catch their prey – anemones and jellyfish. There are also numerous types of marine worms living in sand, mud and holes in rock.

Can you guess which of these animals live by the coast and which ones live in freshwater or inland?

Seven-armed starfish

Snakelocks anemone

Hedgehog

Great crested newt

COMMON STARFISH

Starfish have muscular, spiny arms with thousands of tiny, tube-like feet, with which they seem to glide along. The feet have suckers which grip the starfish's prey before it is devoured.

DID YOU KNOW?
Starfish don't have a brain or blood, but they do have simple eyes. If they lose any arms, they can regrow them!

SHORE:	Rocky
ZONE:	Lower
SEEN:	All year
FEEDS ON:	Seashells and crustaceans
FEATURES:	Five orange, red or purple arms
SIZE:	Up to 50 cm across

CUSHION STAR

These tiny starfish are one of several species of starfish that may be found living in rockpools. Like all starfish, they feed by turning their stomach inside out to pour digestive juices over their prey.

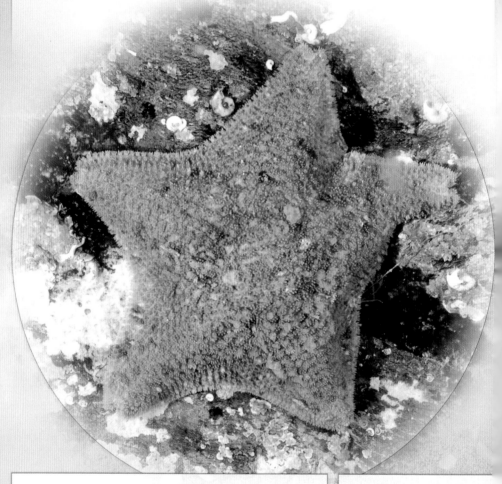

SHORE:	Rocky
ZONE:	Lower
SEEN:	All year
FEEDS ON:	Dead animals and seaweed
FEATURES:	Five stubby green or brown arms
SIZE:	Up to 5 cm across

DID YOU KNOW?
Cushion starfish have many minuscule tube feet. They leave their hiding places at night in order to feed.

SEA URCHIN

These ancient spiny creatures trundle over the seabed grazing on seaweed and eating small animals, sometimes in large herds. You are most likely to see their empty dimpled shells, known as "tests".

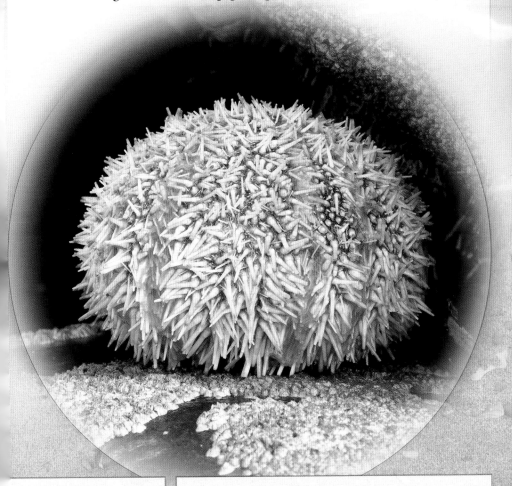

DID YOU KNOW?
A sea urchin's bottom is on its top, and its mouth is underneath! It has five sharp teeth which are self-sharpening.

SHORE:	Rocky with seaweed
ZONE:	Lower
SEEN:	All year round
FEEDS ON:	Mainly seaweed and algae
FEATURES:	Many pale spines
SIZE:	Up to 15 cm across

BEADLET ANEMONE

Sea anemones are animals related to coral. They attach to rocks and have waving tentacles armed with stinging cells. When the tide goes out exposing the anemone to air, its tentacles retract into its body.

SHORE:	Rocky
ZONE:	Upper to lower
SEEN:	All year round
FEEDS ON:	Pieces of floating food
FEATURES:	Red, green or brown
SIZE:	Up to 5 cm high

DID YOU KNOW?
The anemone's stingers sense tiny prey in the water and fire a spear-like structure filled with venom to paralyse it.

STRAWBERRY ANEMONE

This large, pretty anemone lives mainly in rockpools on southern coasts, but as climate change warms our seas, it is spreading rapidly north. Its pale spots might remind you of the pips on strawberries.

DID YOU KNOW?
Sea anemones stick to rocks using a powerful sucker. Their many tentacles are arranged in groups of six.

SHORE:	Rocky
ZONE:	Lower
SEEN:	All year round
FEEDS ON:	Pieces of floating food
FEATURES:	Bright red with pale green spots
SIZE:	Up to 10 cm high

MOON JELLYFISH

Jellyfish are nearly all water and lack a brain or heart. Yet they are superb predators, using the stinging tentacles that dangle from their main body, the "bell". These are Britain's commonest jellyfish.

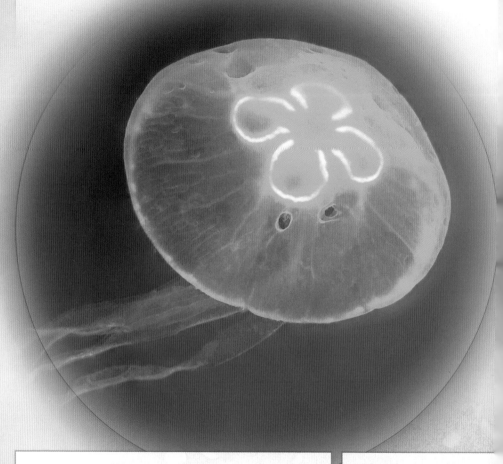

FOUND:	All British coasts
ZONE:	Surface waters
SEEN:	Mainly summer
FEEDS ON:	Tiny floating prey
FEATURES:	Transparent bell with four discs
SIZE:	Usually 15 to 20 cm across

DID YOU KNOW?
Never touch a stranded jellyfish! Moon jellies are harmless, but others can sting – even when they are dead.

OTHER JELLYFISH

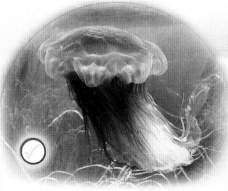

COMPASS JELLYFISH
These jellyfish have a yellowish bell with smart, brown stripes. Several short, frilly arms hang down in the middle, surrounded by longer tentacles which sting.

BLUE JELLYFISH
The adults of this species are an amazing blue colour, though smaller ones may be paler. They appear in summer, attracted by plankton on which they feed.

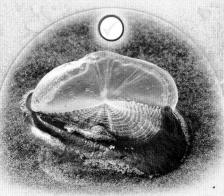

BARREL JELLYFISH
Barrel jellyfish have a chunky, mushroom-shaped bell which can be 80 to 90 cm wide, with eight frilly arms underneath. They are also called dustbin-lid jellyfish!

BY-THE-WIND SAILOR
This is not one but a colony of many sea creatures. The light-blue "sail" catches the wind transporting it to new feeding grounds, or washing it ashore.

HONEYCOMB WORM

Groups of this worm build boulder-like homes along the shore. They make these from grains of sand stuck together, which then harden. The surface is covered in small openings, each with a worm inside.

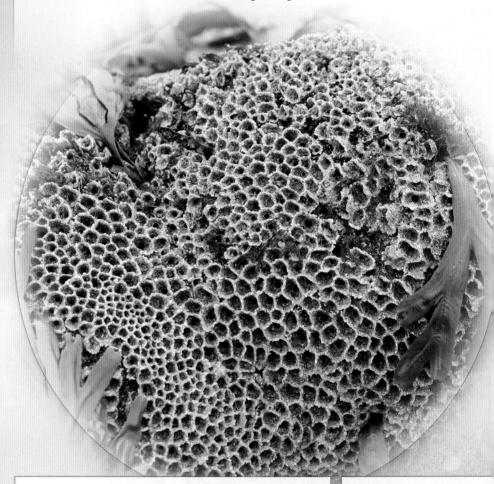

SHORE:	Rocky
ZONE:	Lower
SEEN:	All year round
FEEDS ON:	Food filtered from water
FEATURES:	Builds rock-like colonies
SIZE:	Each worm is 3 to 4 cm long

DID YOU KNOW?
The little tubes the worms live in are six-sided and form a honeycomb pattern all over the colony.

OTHER WORMS

LUGWORM
Lugworms live in U-shaped burrows on sandy beaches. The sand they excavate forms lots of squiggly mounds, which are known as worm casts.

SAND MASON
It is almost impossible to spot these big worms. Look instead for their homes made of tubes of hardened sand sticking up from the level of the beach.

TUBE WORM
Tube worms build tiny spiral shells which look like white spots on seaweeds, rocks and shells. They catch passing food using feathery tentacles.

RAGWORM
Ragworms have so many legs, they look like pink millipedes. They live in burrows on muddy shores, leaving only to mate and lay eggs in the water.

FOSSILS

AMMONITE
Fossils of the beautiful, coiled shells of these ancient sea creatures can be found in soft rocks on beaches, often at the bottom of cliffs.

BELEMNITE
Belemnites were squid-like creatures which lived and died out millions of years ago. Their remains look like small bullets made of stone.

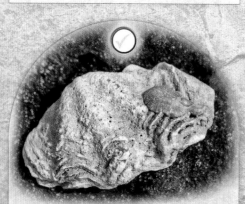

SEASHELL
The seas in ancient times were full of many animals with shells. The soft part of their bodies rotted away, leaving fossils of the shells imprinted in rock.

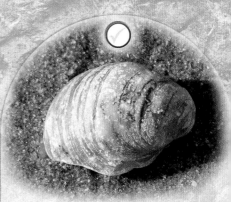

DEVIL'S TOENAIL
These are the fossil shells of extinct oysters. Their name comes from their curved shape, which made people think they were the claws of a giant sea monster!

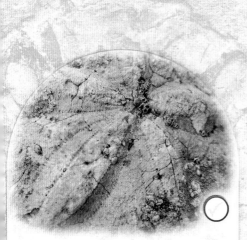

SEA URCHIN
The fossil shells of ancient sea urchins are a great find. Their shells are roughly circular, usually with marks or imprints which form a neat pattern.

SHARK'S TOOTH
Just as sharks do today, the sharks of millions of years ago kept shedding and growing teeth. Fossils of the teeth turn up on many rocky and shingly beaches.

SEA LILY
Sea lilies are underwater animals, not plants as the name suggests. They have been around for millions of years and their fossils are commonly found on beaches.

DINOSAUR FOOTPRINT
Sometimes, the footprints of large dinosaurs are preserved as fossils in rock. These are called trace fossils, and famous finds have been made in Britain.

BIRDS

Coasts are rich feeding grounds for seabirds such as puffins, gannets and gulls. Many nest in noisy groups called colonies, often on cliffs or islands where they are safe from predators. Large numbers of wading birds, ducks and geese find food along beaches and on coastal mud and marshes.

Look out for nesting seabirds like these in spring and summer. Can you match these chicks to their parents?

Herring gull

Eider

Common tern

① ② ③

PUFFIN

A massive, multicoloured beak and waddling walk give the puffin a clown-like appearance in its clifftop colonies. In the sea it is a superb hunter, chasing fish underwater powered by strong, beating wings.

DID YOU KNOW?		
Puffins hold fish in their beak with their spiny tongue so firmly, they can catch more without any others falling out.	FOUND:	Tops of cliffs
	SEEN:	Spring and summer
	FEEDS ON:	Sand eels and other small fish
	FEATURES:	Huge colourful bill; orange feet
	YOUNG:	1 chick
	LENGTH:	26 to 29 cm

RAZORBILL

This seabird's distinctive bill is thicker than that of the similar-looking guillemot, alongside which it often nests on cliff ledges. Its black-and-white plumage makes it look as if it is wearing a dinner jacket.

FOUND: Cliffs

SEEN: Spring and summer

FEEDS ON: Fish such as sand eel and herring

FEATURES: Flat-sided bill with white stripes

YOUNG: 1 chick

LENGTH: 37 to 40 cm

DID YOU KNOW?
Young razorbills leave their nest before they can fly, by leaping off the cliff and tumbling down into the sea below.

GUILLEMOT

During the breeding season, guillemots live in large colonies, squeezed onto narrow ledges of bare rock far above the sea below. The parents lay a single egg, then take it in turns to find fish for their fluffy chick.

DID YOU KNOW?
Every guillemot egg has a unique pattern of blobs and squiggles. This helps the parent birds spot their precious egg.

FOUND:	Cliffs
SEEN:	Spring and summer
FEEDS ON:	Small fish; crustaceans
FEATURES:	Brown and white with pointed bill
YOUNG:	1 chick
LENGTH:	38 to 45 cm

CORMORANT

Cormorants have a long, snake-like neck and dark feathers. Unlike that of other birds, their plumage becomes soggy during dives for fish, so they sit for long periods with their wings outstretched to dry out.

FOUND:	All coasts
SEEN:	All year round
FEEDS ON:	Medium-sized fish
FEATURES:	Hooked beak; long neck
YOUNG:	2 to 4 chicks
LENGTH:	80 to 94 cm

DID YOU KNOW?
Cormorants can be seen in salt- and freshwater. They build big, untidy nests on low cliffs and in large trees by water.

GANNET

Gannets diving for fish splash headfirst into the sea at up to 60 mph, and are a wildlife spectacle. Special air sacs in the head and neck cushion these elegant birds against the massive impact of the water.

DID YOU KNOW?
The largest colonies of gannets are on cliffs in Yorkshire and on rocky islands off the Welsh and Scottish coasts.

FOUND:	Mostly at sea
SEEN:	Mainly spring and summer
FEEDS ON:	Fish such as mackerel
FEATURES:	Dagger-shaped bill; black wingtips
YOUNG:	1 chick
LENGTH:	90 to 100 cm

FULMAR

The fulmar spends most of its life at sea, returning to land only to breed. It is related to albatrosses and, like them, has a pair of tubes on its bill to remove the excess salt it picks up as it dives for fish.

FOUND:	Cliffs and at sea
SEEN:	All year round
FEEDS ON:	Fish and squid
FEATURES:	Heavy bill with tubes on top
YOUNG:	1 chick
LENGTH:	45 to 50 cm

DID YOU KNOW?
Nesting fulmars will squirt disgusting, foul-smelling stomach juices from their beaks at predators. So watch out!

LESSER BLACK-BACKED GULL

Loud and confident, this bird is happy to eat anything it can find, either at sea or on land. It is slightly smaller than the similar herring gull, and has yellow legs and a darker-grey back and wings.

DID YOU KNOW?
Many of these gulls migrate south to the coasts of Portugal, Spain and North Africa for the autumn and winter.

FOUND:	Coasts, rooftops, shingle beaches
SEEN:	Mainly spring and summer
FEEDS ON:	Fish, squid, seashells, worms, scraps
FEATURES:	Bright yellow legs and bill
YOUNG:	Usually 2 or 3 chicks
LENGTH:	52 to 62 cm

HERRING GULL

The herring gull's harsh, honking cries are a classic sound of the seaside. It is bold enough to steal food from other birds and people, and raid litter bins. It often builds its nest on buildings.

FOUND:	Coasts, rooftops, shingle beaches
SEEN:	All year round
FEEDS ON:	Fish, squid, seashells, worms, scraps
FEATURES:	Bright yellow bill; pink legs
YOUNG:	Usually 2 or 3 chicks
LENGTH:	55 to 67 cm

DID YOU KNOW?
This is a young herring gull. Adults have red spots on their beaks, which chicks peck when wanting to be fed.

OTHER GULLS

GREAT BLACK-BACKED GULL

All these gulls are slightly different: this one has a large bill and dark wings. It preys on the chicks of other seabirds.

KITTIWAKE

One of the smaller gulls, the kittiwake has a pointed lemon-yellow bill and black legs. It is named after its "kitti-WAAK" cry and nests on sea-cliff ledges.

BLACK-HEADED GULL

This small gull has a dark brown (not black) head in summer and an almost white head in winter after it has moulted. It is found as much inland as by the coast.

COMMON GULL

Its greenish-yellow bill and legs are the best way to identify this bird, which is not that common. Like the black-headed gull, it is also seen inland.

COMMON TERN

Terns were once known as sea swallows because of their long, pointed wings, forked tails and graceful flight style. They are often spotted a short distance from the shore, where they dive for fish.

FOUND:	All coasts; nests on shingle beaches
SEEN:	Spring and summer
FEEDS ON:	Small fish
FEATURES:	Red bill; large black area in wing
YOUNG:	3 or 4 chicks
LENGTH:	31 to 35 cm

DID YOU KNOW?
Terns nest in a scrape on the ground, where their fluffy chicks are camouflaged against the pebbles and shingle.

ARCTIC TERN

These terns migrate further than any other bird on Earth. Each year, having spent the winter months in the Southern Ocean as far south as Antarctica, they travel to northern parts of the world to breed.

DID YOU KNOW?
Most Arctic terns nest in northern Britain and Ireland, on small islands offshore where there are no land predators.

FOUND: All coasts; nests on shingle beaches
SEEN: Spring and summer
FEEDS ON: Small fish
FEATURES: Red bill; a little black on wings
YOUNG: 3 or 4 chicks
LENGTH: 33 to 35 cm

WADING BIRDS

SANDERLING

Flocks of these energetic little birds race up and down sandy shores. Non-breeding adults, like this one, have grey backs and breeding birds have brown ones.

TURNSTONE

Turnstones do exactly as their name suggests: they flick stones over to look for food hiding underneath. Listen out for their repeated chuckling calls.

OYSTERCATCHER

These eye-catching birds use their long beaks to hammer or stab seashells to reach the creatures inside. They are found on the coast and inland.

CURLEW

Thanks to their hugely long, curved bill, curlews can reach deep into wet sand and mud to find animals buried beyond the reach of other birds.

REDSHANK
Redshanks are nervous birds and are usually the first to fly off if they see people or dogs. Their bright orange-red legs are a common sight wading in mud.

RINGED PLOVER
This little wading bird likes pebbly and shingly beaches. It has a short bill, so picks small items from the surface of the beach, running to catch them.

AVOCET
Avocets have a unique bill that curves upwards, which they sweep from side to side through shallow water to trap food. Their numbers have been increasing.

DUNLIN
One of the most abundant small wading birds in Britain, the dunlin forms large flocks on muddy shores in winter. Some contain many thousands of birds.

SHELDUCK

The shelduck is nearly the size of a goose. In summer, pairs guide
their broods of ducklings across shallow pools and marshy areas.
Later, broods merge to form larger flocks, guarded by several adults.

FOUND: Muddy shores and coastal marshes

SEEN: All year round

FEEDS ON: Marine worms, shells and snails

FEATURES: Male's red beak has a lump on top

YOUNG: 8 to 10 chicks

LENGTH: 60 to 65 cm

DID YOU KNOW?
*Shelducks often nest
underground inside old
rabbit burrows. They are
very protective parents
and will chase off gulls.*

EIDER

Eiders are able to brave the sea in all weathers. The brown females line their nests with fluffy, supersoft feathers called down, plucked from their breast. Males, like this one, have black and white plumage.

DID YOU KNOW?
In winter and spring, male eiders make strange, throaty cooing calls, which is how they attract females.

FOUND: Rocky coasts and islands
SEEN: All year round
FEEDS ON: Mussels and other shellfish
FEATURES: Males have green on their necks
YOUNG: Usually 4 to 5 chicks
LENGTH: 50 to 65 cm

BRENT GOOSE
These small, dark-plumaged geese migrate to British and Irish coasts for the winter. Groups of them may be seen feeding on eel-grass and seaweed.

BARNACLE GOOSE
Winter visitors from the Arctic, these geese feed on grass and grain in fields, and at night fly to coastal mudflats for safety. Their calls sound like yapping dogs.

RAVEN
You can identify our largest species of crow by its size, diamond-shaped tail and harsh "kronk-kronk" cries. Pairs enjoy tumbling in the air together.

JACKDAW
These are small crows with a grey neck patch. Their "chack chack" calls will grab your attention, and you will sometimes see them in large flocks.

PEREGRINE FALCON
The world's fastest bird, the peregrine may hit 200 mph during vertical dives through the air, chasing after prey such as pigeons and crows.

ROCK PIPIT
This sparrow-sized bird creeps around the boulders, cliffs and seaweed of rocky coasts, where its plumage helps it to blend in. Look for its white tail feathers.

KESTREL
Kestrels hunt voles and mice by hovering in mid-air over long grass, then dropping to catch them. You see them hunting along clifftops or on marshes.

LINNET
Linnets can be seen perched in bushes and areas of gorse along coasts, or searching for seeds on the ground. Males have a rosy breast and forehead.

MAMMALS

Our long coastline attracts several dozen kinds of sea mammal. Coasts are the best habitat to spot otters, and seals use beaches to rest and give birth. You might also catch sight of dolphins, porpoises and even whales, which visit sheltered bays and shallow waters to feed.

Do you know which of these mammals are more often seen on and from the seashore and which are usually seen inland?

Fox

Rabbit

House mouse

Orca

OTTER

Otters are carnivores related to weasels, and are equally happy on land and in water. Their streamlined bodies, waterproof fur and webbed feet make them graceful, athletic swimmers.

DID YOU KNOW?
Otters dive frequently, but must surface to breathe. They build underground nests, which are called holts.

FOUND: Quiet rocky shores
SEEN: All year round
FEEDS ON: Fish, octopus, crustaceans
FEATURES: Sleek brown body; long tail
YOUNG: 2 or 3 cubs
LENGTH: Up to 80 cm (without the tail)

COMMON DOLPHIN

These dolphins live out at sea in "pods" of around 20 animals. They swim fast and are playful, often following boats and jumping in the waves. You may spot them from ferries and on boat trips.

FOUND:	All coasts, except in the east
SEEN:	Mainly summer
FEEDS ON:	Fish – herring, sardine, mackerel
FEATURES:	Curved dorsal fin; pale patch
YOUNG:	1 calf
LENGTH:	1.7 to 2.5 m

DID YOU KNOW?
Common dolphins can swim at speeds of up to 30 mph and hold their breath underwater for about 10 minutes.

BOTTLENOSE DOLPHIN

Named for their stubby beaks, bottlenose dolphins are a large species which make acrobatic leaps high in the air. Groups of them may be found close to the shore and can even be spotted from some beaches.

DID YOU KNOW?
These dolphins enjoy body-surfing at the surface of the sea and sometimes smack their tails hard on the water.

FOUND: Northern and western coasts
SEEN: All year round
FEEDS ON: Fish and squid
FEATURES: Large, without pale areas
YOUNG: 1 calf
LENGTH: Up to 4 m

HARBOUR PORPOISE

Much smaller than dolphins, porpoises swim more slowly and are shy. As they do not leap clear of the water, you will usually see just the small triangular fin on their back as they surface.

FOUND: All coasts
SEEN: All year round
FEEDS ON: Fish and squid
FEATURES: Small stubby dorsal fin on its back
YOUNG: 1 calf
LENGTH: 1.5 to 1.7 m

DID YOU KNOW?
Porpoises are usually sighted alone or in twos or threes. They can be seen close to the coast, avoiding noisy places.

MINKE WHALE

This whale (pronounced "minky") has a long pointed head and massive jaws. It is a type of baleen whale – ones that have frilled plates instead of teeth, which filter food from large gulps of seawater.

DID YOU KNOW?
Minke whales occasionally leap out of the water, or breach, probably to send signals to other whales.

FOUND:	Northern and western coasts
SEEN:	Mainly summer
FEEDS ON:	Fish and squid
FEATURES:	Very long, streamlined body
YOUNG:	1 calf
LENGTH:	7 to 10 m

GREY SEAL

From September to December, pregnant females haul themselves on to the shore to give birth to their young pups. The scientific name for grey seal – *Halichoerus grypus* – means sea pig with a hooked nose.

FOUND:	All coasts
SEEN:	All year round
FEEDS ON:	Fish
FEATURES:	Long nose; nostrils do not touch
YOUNG:	1 pup
LENGTH:	1.8 to 2.6 m

DID YOU KNOW?
Grey seals' sensitive whiskers detect fish 100 m away. Male grey seals, or bulls, can weigh a hefty 300 kg.

COMMON SEAL

Also called a harbour seal, this species has its pups in June and July at a handful of wide, sandy beaches – the same ones every year. The young pups can swim within a few hours of being born.

DID YOU KNOW?	

A mother common seal's milk is very rich, being nearly 50% fat, so her pup doubles its weight within four weeks.

FOUND:	All coasts, except southwest Britain
SEEN:	All year round
FEEDS ON:	Fish and squid
FEATURES:	Short nose; nostrils meet in a "V"
YOUNG:	1 pup
LENGTH:	1.3 to 1.9 m

SEAWEED

Seaweeds are living things known as marine algae. Scientists group them into three types: green, brown and red. Their ribbon-like or bushy parts are known as fronds, and most have some kind of anchor, called a holdfast, to secure them to rocks or to the seabed.

Do you know which two of the six organisms shown below are common types of seaweed?

Catkins

Bracken

Lichen

Lords-and-ladies

Fucus

Dulse

KELP

The name kelp applies to several species of large, brown algae, and many sea creatures take shelter or hunt among their long fronds. This is golden kelp, which can be found off the south-west coast of Britain.

DID YOU KNOW?

Kelp grows very quickly and forms great forests underwater. It is easiest to see at low tide, when its fronds are exposed.

SHORE:	Rocky
ZONE:	Lower
SEEN:	All year round
COLOUR:	Different shades of brown
FEATURES:	Flat fronds with long stalks
LENGTH:	Up to 4.5 m

BLADDER WRACK

The leathery fronds of bladder wrack usually have pale pockets, or bladders, of air bubbles arranged in pairs. They help the seaweed to rise and fall with the tides, pulling it upright to absorb sunlight.

SHORE:	Rocky
ZONE:	Middle
SEEN:	All year round
COLOUR:	Olive-brown
FEATURES:	Wavy fronds with pockets of air
LENGTH:	Up to 1 m

DID YOU KNOW?
Plants produce oxygen – and marine plants, which include seaweeds, make over half of Earth's oxygen.

CORAL WEED

Thick clumps of this pinkish-red seaweed look and feel like coral. The fronds have feathery branches and are stiff, because they contain the mineral calcium carbonate. Coral weed is often found in rockpools.

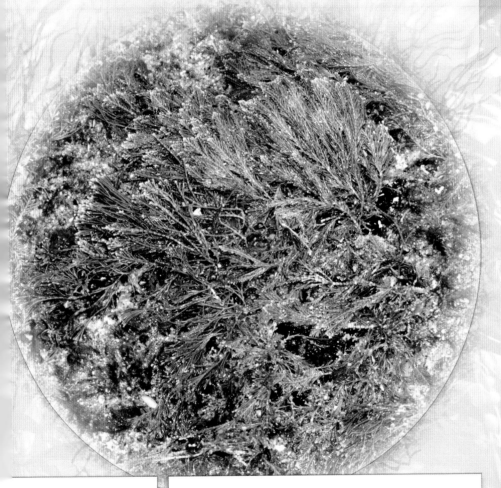

DID YOU KNOW?
Coral weed forms a colourful layer in the bottom of rockpools. Small sea creatures hide amongst its fronds.

SHORE:	Rocky
ZONE:	Middle
SEEN:	All year round
COLOUR:	Pinkish-red
FEATURES:	Fronds are short, stiff and branched
LENGTH:	Up to 12 cm

OARWEED
Oarweed is a species of kelp with shiny brown fronds that end in wavy ribbons. It grows up to 2 metres long and lives on the lowest part of rocky coasts.

CHANNELLED WRACK
This seaweed lives on rocks that are uncovered at low tide. The sides of its fronds curl inwards to create a channel down the middle, which stores water.

SUGAR KELP
This kelp grows in shallow water, where its dense fronds form a submerged forest. It is wide and frilly, and people used to gather it to add to soups or stews.

LAVER
This seaweed of the rocky shore can be olive-green, brown or purple. It is edible, with a salty flavour, and is traditionally harvested in Wales.

IRISH MOSS
This is common on rocky shores, including in rockpools, and is harvested on a large scale to produce a thick gel used in many foods, including icecream.

SEA LETTUCE
As its name suggests, this low-growing seaweed is edible. Its green fronds are so bright and vibrant, they seem almost to glow in the shallow water of rockpools.

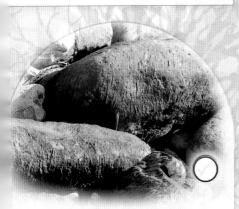

GUTWEED
Gutweed spreads out over rocks or sand, where it looks like green slime. You will find it all over the shore and in rockpools during spring and summer.

VELVET HORN
This green seaweed is soft and spongy. Look for it along Britain's western coasts, particularly on the lower part of the shore and in rockpools.

PLANTS

To survive on the seashore, plants need to be able to cope with the salty air and the sandy or rocky ground. These things make life difficult, but a variety of plants flourish here. They offer valuable food for insects and help to protect the coast, preventing it from being washed away in storms.

Do you know which of the organisms shown below are plants and which of them are fungi?

Gorse

Heather

Jelly ear

Fly agaric

Harebell

Sulphur tuft

THRIFT

In late spring and early summer, the baby-pink pompoms of thrift flowers add a splash of colour to sea-cliff tops and the grassy parts of salt marshes. The plant's tough leaves form a springy green cushion.

DID YOU KNOW?	
Some seabirds like to nest among clumps of thrift. It is also commonly grown in garden rockeries.	

NATIVE TO:	Britain and rest of Europe
FOUND:	Cliffs and salt marshes
ZONE:	Upper
FEATURES:	Pink flowerheads; thin leaves
FLOWERS:	May to July
HEIGHT:	15 to 30 cm

SEA HOLLY

Spiky leaves give this plant its name. It is not a type of holly tree; it is actually a member of the carrot family. The thick and waxy leaves help it to cope with salty sea breezes, and its fat roots store water.

NATIVE TO:	Britain and the rest of Europe
FOUND:	Sand dunes
ZONE:	Upper
FEATURES:	Spiky leaves; pale purple flowers
FLOWERS:	July to September
HEIGHT:	30 to 90 cm

DID YOU KNOW?
Sea holly is able to grow in pure sand. In medieval times, its thick roots were dug up and turned into a snack.

SEA BEET

Sea beet grows around the coast on beaches, mudflats and sand dunes. Its glossy, bright green leaves are a healthy food, which taste similar to spinach.

MARSH SAMPHIRE

This plant is found on muddy estuaries and salt marshes. Its stems, which feel soft and squidgy, can be harvested in summer and taste very salty.

SEA KALE

Look for this member of the cabbage family at the top of shingle and pebble beaches. It has squeaky leaves and is adorned with white flowers in summer.

ALEXANDERS

Alexanders thrives along coastal paths and roadsides. The glossy leaves are grouped in threes, and in April and May it has large clusters of yellow-green flowers.

WILD-FLOWER GALLERY

SEA ASTERS

Loved by butterflies, sea asters have purple petals and a daisy-like golden centre. The flowers appear unusually late in the year, between July and September.

YELLOW-HORNED POPPY

The vibrant flowers of this plant brighten shingle shores and sand dunes in summer. After flowering, long green seedpods appear, which look like curved horns!

SEA BINDWEED

This plant's shiny, heart-shaped leaves creep over beaches, and trail over walls along the seafront. The huge flowers are shaped like the end of a trumpet.

VIPER'S BUGLOSS

This bright blue wild flower lights up sand dunes and gravelly areas by the coast. Insects adore its nectar. People believed this plant cured venomous snake bites!

SEA CAMPION

The white flowers of sea campion appear in summer on cliff ledges and along shingle beaches. Every petal is split neatly in two, and there is a bulge below the flower.

SEA LAVENDER

With sprays of beautiful purple flowers all summer long, this lavender can be found on muddy coasts and salt marshes everywhere except Scotland.

SPRING SQUILL

For a small plant, spring quill has a big impact. In April and May, when there are few other seaside flowers around, its pale-blue star-shaped flowers really stand out.

RED VALERIAN

The bright pinkish-red flowers of red valerian attract many insects, especially moths and butterflies. It grows in rocky places and is in bloom for a long time.

MARRAM GRASS

Many coastal sand dunes would be blown or washed away were it not for clumps of this special grass. A dense network of roots holds the sand in place, helping to protect this fragile habitat.

NATIVE TO:	Britain and rest of Europe
FOUND:	Sand dunes
ZONE:	Upper
FEATURES:	Tufts of long, sharp-edged leaves
FLOWERS:	July and August
HEIGHT:	Up to 1 m

DID YOU KNOW?
Marram grass helps to shelter other smaller plants from the wind, and provides a home for rare sand lizards.

TREES & BUSHES

SEA BUCKTHORN

This thorny bush grows in thickets on sand dunes and low cliffs. In September and October it has masses of orange berries — a welcome feast for hungry birds.

TAMARISK

In Britain, this bushy tree is often planted on sand dunes and in coastal gardens as a windbreak. It can withstand hot, dry conditions and strong sea winds.

CORSICAN PINE

Originally from the Mediterranean, this tree is now a common sight on our coasts. Its spiky evergreen needles can be longer than fingers!

SCOTS PINE

This is Britain and Ireland's only native pine tree. It copes well with the sandy soil of coasts, and has evergreen needles, pointy cones and an orangey-pink bark.

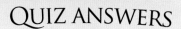

QUIZ ANSWERS

CRUSTACEANS
The two crustaceans are the sea slater and the lobster.

•

SHELLS
All the animals shown feed on shellfish, except for the turkey.

•

FISH
Only the dolphins are mammals; all the rest are fish.

•

OTHER SEA ANIMALS
The coastal creatures are the seven-armed starfish and the snakelocks anemone. The inland animals are the great crested newt and the hedgehog.

•

BIRDS
These are the young of the following birds:
1. Eider 2. Common tern 3. Herring gull

•

MAMMALS
The orca is most likely to be seen from the coast, and the rabbit is common around sand dunes and coastal grassy areas. The house mouse and the fox are found inland.

•

SEAWEED
The two types of seaweed are dulse and fucus.

•

PLANTS
The fungi are the jelly ear, sulphur tuft and fly agaric. The plants are the gorse, the heather and the harebell.

ACKNOWLEDGEMENTS

GUEST AUTHOR: Ben Hoare

Scientific adviser: Heather Buttivant

Production adviser: Yolanta Motylinska

Editor: Katie Crous • Proofreader: Penny Phillips

Prepress designer: Les Hunt

Foreign rights: Odette Lusby, Boundless Books 4 All

PICTURE CREDITS

© Shutterstock

p5 Velvet swimming crab: davemhuntphotography; Edible crab: Alex Stemmers; Spider crab: Becky Gill; p6 Brown shrimp: slowmotiongli; p7 Prawn: Macronatura.es; p8 Oystercatcher: imageBROKER.com; Black-throated diver: Erni; Humpback whale: Craig Lambert Photography; Sea turtle: Been there YB; p12 Mussels: Ginny Sturdy; p13 Tellin: Images01; p14 Periwinkle: valda butterworth; p15 Dog whelk: Dan Bagur; p16 Goose barnacle: jflin98; p18 Perch: Nikitin Victor; Pike: Rostislav Stefanek; Brown trout and Carp: Eric Isselee; Mackerel: Good luck images; Dolphins: Joost van Uffelen; p19 Basking shark: Martin Prochazkacz; p20 Blenny: ABS Natural History; p21 Sand goby: Dan_Manila; p22 Butterfish: nanadou; p23 Grey mullet: Gerald Robert Fischer; Rock goby: Gennaro DiBs; Dab: coxy58; p24 Snakelock anemone: Greg Amptman; Seven-armed starfish: valda butterworth; Newt: WitR; p26 Cushion star: LABETAA Andre; p27 Urchin: davemhuntphotography; p29 Anemone: Becky Gill; p30 Moon jellyfish: Camilla Blaschuk; p31 Compass jellyfish: Becky Gill; Blue jellyfish: ABS Natural History; Barrel jellyfish: Damsea; By-the-wind sailor: Badon Hill Studio; p32 Honeycomb worm: Fencewood Studio; p33 Sandmason: J Need; Tube worm: ChWeiss; Ragworm: ABS Natural History; p34 Ammonite: Damian Pawlos; Belemnite: Karsten_1; Seashell: Arina_B; p35 Sea urchin: Hvarts; Shark's tooth: SRRPProductions; Sea lily: Roger de la Harpe; Dinosaur footprint: Christine Dodd; p36 Eider: Bernd Wolter; Common tern: Amanda Guercio; Eider chick: Stephan Morris; Tern chick: Pikkymaster; Herring-gull chick: Rudmer Zwerver; p38 Razorbill: David Osborn; p39 Guillemot: Piotr Poznan; p40 Cormorant: Menno Schaefer; p41 Gannet: David Osborn; p42 Fulmar: Jeremy Richards; p45 Kittiwake: CezaryKorkosz; Common gull: Erni; p46 Common tern: Wirestock Creators; p47 Arctic tern: LouieLea; p48 Sanderling: M Huston; p49 Redshank: David Osborn; Ringed plover: Dave Montreuil; Dunlin: Sandra Standbridge; p50 Shelduck: NABA CHOUDHURY; p51 Eider: AndreAnita; p52 Brent goose: ShayneKayePhoto; Raven: Glenn McCrea; Jackdaw: A G Baxter; p53 Peregrine falcon: kojihirano; Rock pipit: gergosz; Kestrel: Andy Wasley; Linnet: Israel Hervas Bengochea; p54 Fox: Milan Zygmunt; Orca: Tory Kallman; House mouse: Ihor Hvozdetskyi; p56 Common dolphin: niall dunne; p57 Bottlenose dolphin: Tory Kallman; p58 Harbour porpoise: Tom Middleton; p59 Minke whale: Islandjems - Jemma Craig; p60 Grey seal: David Osborn; p63 Golden kelp: Damsea; p64 Bladder wrack: Giles Kent; p65 Coral weed: Brian Maudsley; p66 Oarweed: liz seymour; Channelled wrack: ChWeiss; Sugar kelp: ANGHI; Laver: Chris Moody; p67 Sea lettuce: R. Knapp; Velvet horn: Damsea; p68 Heather: Martin Fowler; Sulphur tuft: arenysam; p70 Sea holly: Carlos Neto; p71 Sea beet: Andrew Chisholm; Marsh samphire: Oxie99; p72 Sea asters: goran_safarek; Sea bindweed: ID-VIDEO; p73 Sea lavender: Danny Hummel; Spring squill: Andrew Roland; p75 Tamarisk: LutsenkoLarissa

Icon images

Crustaceans; shells; fish; other marine animals; mammals; seaweed: LynxVector

Birds: Sparrowbh; Plants: iana

p15 Spotted cowries © Louis Hagger

p5 Hermit crab; p23 Sand eels © Heather Buttivant

All other photos © Fine Feather Press

WARNING!
Please do not collect or eat any of the plants or animals
that you spot outside as they may be protected – or poisonous.

First published in 2023 by Fine Feather Press Limited
The Coach House, Elstead Road, Farnham, Surrey GU10 1JE
EU enquiries: Andrea Pinnington, 2022 Route de Laurélie
12270 Bor-et-Bar, France
Copyright © 2023 Fine Feather Press Limited

2 4 6 8 10 9 7 5 3 1

A CIP catalogue record is available from the British Library
ISBN: 978-1-908489-70-8
Printed in China

Fine Feather Press Ltd makes every effort to ensure that the papers
used in its books are made from trees that have been legally
sourced from well-managed and credibly certified forests.

www.finefeatherpress.com

NATURE SPOTTERS

CERTIFICATE

AWARDED TO

FOR FINDING

50

SEASHORE
ANIMALS & PLANTS